STEADY HAND, QUIET MIND

Stoic Wisdom for the Working Artist

Design gives clarity. Story gives meaning. Freshness gives life.

Inspired by the Meditations of Marcus Aurelius

By Steve Puttrich

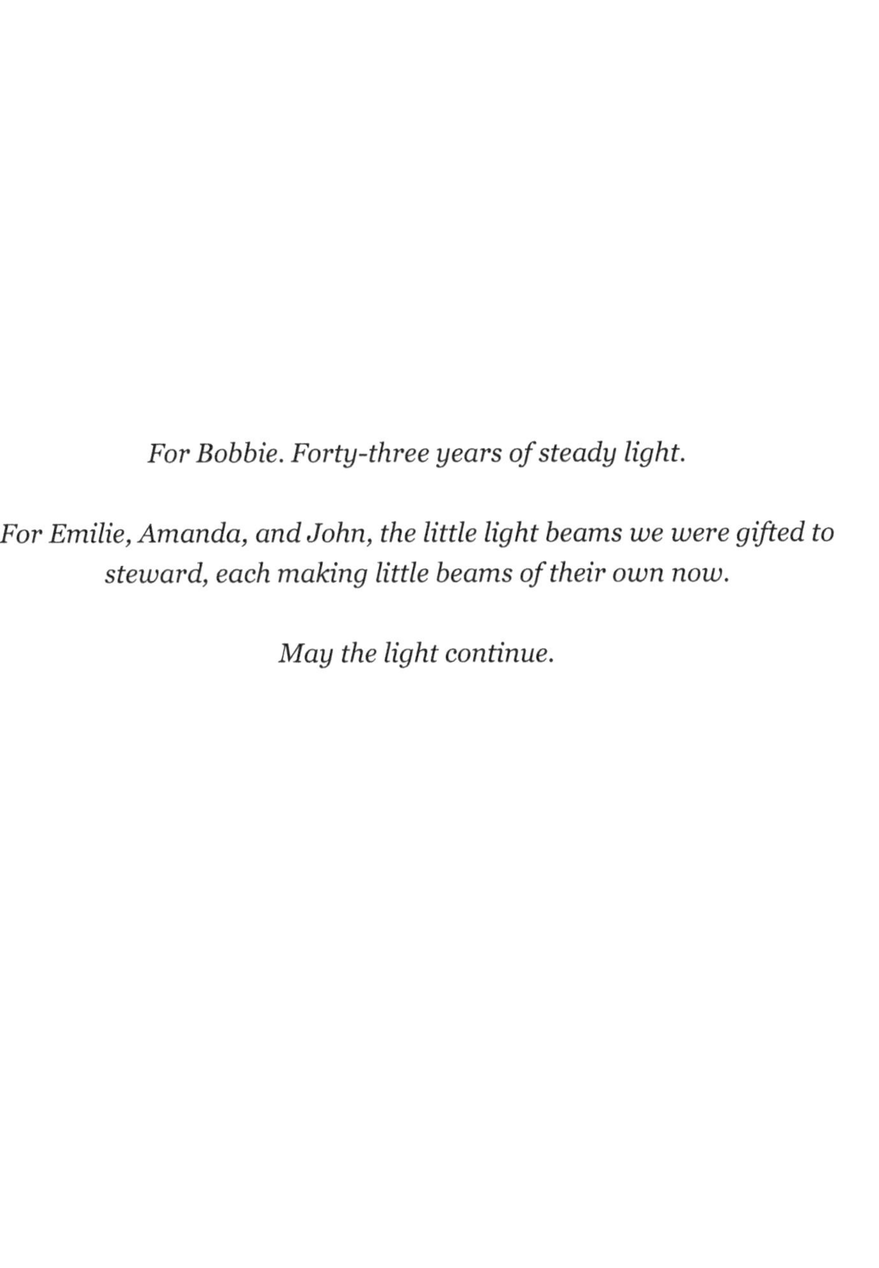

For Bobbie. Forty-three years of steady light.

For Emilie, Amanda, and John, the little light beams we were gifted to steward, each making little beams of their own now.

May the light continue.

Table of Contents

Foreword

A Note Before We Begin

This book started the way most useful things start: with a problem I couldn't solve by painting harder.

I had been working as an artist and teacher for decades. I knew how to mix color. I knew how to design a composition. I could run a workshop, set up a plein air easel in wind that would knock over a lesser tripod, and talk about value structure until everyone in the room either understood it or pretended to.

But the inner game was another thing entirely.

I kept hitting the same walls. Comparison with other painters who seemed to have what I didn't. Fear of starting a piece that might go wrong. The quiet ache of putting good work into the world and hearing nothing back. Overworking paintings because I didn't trust myself to stop. Letting criticism rattle me longer than it should. Letting praise inflate me more than it deserved.

I wasn't looking for self-help. I was looking for steadiness.

Then I picked up Meditations by Marcus Aurelius. Not because someone told me to, but because I'd heard it described as a journal a man wrote to himself in the middle of a war, trying to stay sane and do his job well. That sounded familiar. Not the war part. The staying sane part.

What I found in those pages wasn't cold philosophy. It was a man talking to himself the way a good teacher talks to a struggling student: directly, honestly, without sentimentality, but with real kindness underneath. He was writing himself reminders. Simple ones. Do the work. Let go of what you can't control. Don't chase applause. Be useful. Pay attention. Remember that time is short.

I started applying those ideas to my studio life. Then to my teaching. Then to the way I handled the business side of being an artist. And slowly, things got clearer. Not easier. Clearer.

There is something more I should name here, because it runs through the whole book. For many artists, making art is not merely a private act of self-expression. It is also a response. A way of paying attention. A way of honoring what has been given. The ability to see deeply, to be moved by light, by gesture, by weather, by the dignity of ordinary things, is not small. It is a gift. And gifts ask for stewardship.

That word matters. To see your work as stewardship is to remember that your eye, your time, your craft, your influence, even your desire to make something honest and beautiful, are not just possessions to exploit. They are things to tend faithfully. That changes the spirit of the studio. It lowers the fever of self-importance. It steadies ambition. It deepens gratitude.

This book is my attempt to pass that clarity along.

It is not a summary of Stoicism. It's not a Roman history lesson. It's a set of ideas drawn from Marcus Aurelius and translated into the language of paint, light, landscape, and the daily discipline of making art that means something.

If you are a painter, a sculptor, a printmaker, a teacher, or anyone who has ever stood in front of a blank surface and felt both the pull of possibility and the weight of doubt, this book is for you.

Read it slowly. Keep it near your easel. Come back to the chapters that hit hardest. And then do the only thing that matters: pick up the brush and get to work.

Introduction

Why Marcus Aurelius Still Matters to Artists

Somewhere around the year 170 AD, in a military tent on the frozen banks of the Danube, a tired man sat down to write. He was not writing a book. He was not writing for an audience. He was writing to himself. Reminders, corrections, encouragements. Trying to hold his mind together while everything around him demanded more than he thought he had to give.

That man was Marcus Aurelius, Emperor of Rome. And the journal he kept, which we now call Meditations, became one of the most quietly powerful books in the history of Western thought.

Marcus did not write about painting. He wrote about endurance, about self-command, about doing your work without needing the world to notice. He wrote about the trap of ego, the poison of complaint, the discipline of returning to first principles when everything gets complicated. He wrote about mortality, not to be grim, but to be awake. And he did all of it in plain, honest language that still reads like a letter from a friend who happens to be wiser than you.

What does any of this have to do with painting?

Everything.

Because the hardest part of being an artist is not mixing the right color or getting the drawing accurate or learning to handle a palette knife. Those things are learnable. They yield to practice. The hardest part is everything that happens between your ears.

Every serious painter knows the enemies. Distraction: the thousand interruptions that pull you away from the easel before you've done anything worth doing. Comparison: the scrolling sickness of looking at other people's best work and measuring it against your worst. Fear: the paralyzing suspicion that the next painting will prove you're not as good as you hoped. Ego: the small, hungry voice that makes the work about you instead of about the work. Overwork: the refusal to trust a painting and let it breathe. Inconsistency: the habit of painting in bursts and then disappearing for weeks. Discouragement: the slow erosion of belief when the world doesn't respond the way you thought it should.

Marcus Aurelius fought every one of those battles. Not with paint, but with power, duty, loss, and exhaustion. And the strategies he wrote down for himself are as useful to an artist standing at an easel as they were to an emperor standing at the edge of a war.

This is not a book about Stoicism as a formal philosophy. You will not find lengthy explanations of Epictetus or Seneca here. This is a working book for working artists. It takes the strongest, most durable ideas from Meditations and translates them into the language of paint, design, light, studio practice, and the daily discipline of making something true.

The framework I use in my own teaching and painting maps naturally onto stoic thinking. Design gives clarity. It is the structure that holds everything together, the value plan, the composition, the bones of the painting. Stoics believed in order, in seeing things as they are, in stripping away the unnecessary. That is design. Story gives meaning. It is the reason the painting exists: what it says, what it makes you feel, what truth it carries. Marcus wrote constantly about purpose, about aligning your actions with what matters most. That is story. Freshness gives life. It is the mark of a painter who is present, not overworking, not copying, not going through the motions, but responding to the subject with confidence and honesty. Marcus wrote about waking up, about paying attention, about not wasting the hours you have been given. That is freshness. Underneath all three of these ideas sits something even more foundational.

First principles are the foundations that everything else is built on. In painting, they are value, shape, edges, color, and design. They do not change with fashion. They do not expire. They are as true for a painter working today as they were for Velázquez. First principles thinking means that when confusion enters the room, when a painting is failing and you cannot figure out why, you do not reach for a new trick or a fancier brush. You go back to the foundation and ask the simplest questions. Is my value structure working? Are my shapes clear? Are my edges doing their job? Is the design leading the eye where it needs to go? Nine times out of ten, the answer is there. Not in some advanced technique you have not yet learned, but in a basic principle you stopped paying attention to. Marcus Aurelius did the same thing with his own thinking. When life got complicated, he did not reach for more complexity. He returned to what he already knew was true and rebuilt from there.

But there is another layer to this book, and it should be named early. For many artists, making art is more than craft, more than career, more than self-expression. It is also a response. A way of answering the world. The ability to see beauty, feel meaning, notice light, sense story, or be moved by the quiet dignity of ordinary things is not something to treat lightly. It is a gift. And gifts ask something of us. They ask stewardship.

That word matters because it rescues the artist from two dead ends. The first is ego, where the work becomes mainly a way of proving the self. The second is drift, where the work becomes disconnected from purpose and slowly thins into habit, appetite, or noise. Stewardship offers a better path. It says your eye, your craft, your time, your voice, your students, your years are not merely things to spend however you please. They are things to tend. To refine. To offer back with honesty and gratitude.

Here is what I want you to take from these pages: the inner life of the artist matters. Your habits of mind shape your paintings more than your habits of hand. If you can learn to govern your thoughts, to direct your attention, to work without needing constant approval, to simplify, to endure, and to stay honest, your paintings will show it. And your life will be better for it.

You do not need to become a philosopher to benefit from philosophy. You just need to be willing to think clearly about the things that make your art life harder than it needs to be, and to do something about them.

Marcus Aurelius was not a painter. But he was a man who believed that the quality of your work depends on the quality of your mind, that discipline is a form of respect for the gift you've been given, and that the world does not owe you recognition for doing what you were made to do. If that sounds like the kind of teacher you'd want to study under, read on.

A note about how this book works. Each chapter takes a single principle from Marcus Aurelius and translates it into the language of art making. You will find short opening scenes drawn from studio and field experience. You will find the principle stated in plain English. You will find practical applications for painting, teaching, and the business of being an artist. And at the end of each chapter, you will find a few questions worth sitting with. Not exam questions, but journal prompts for a painter who wants to think more clearly about the life he or she is building.

You do not need to read this book in order. If you are in the middle of a creative drought, go to Chapter 11 first. If you are struggling with ego, go to Chapter 5. If you are about to teach a workshop, go to Chapter 10. The chapters are designed to stand on their own. Read the one you need today.

CHAPTER 1
The Inner Citadel

Governing Your Own Mind

The studio is quiet. The light is good. You've got two hours and a subject that interests you. Everything you need is within arm's reach.

And yet, twenty minutes in, your mind is somewhere else. You're thinking about an email you forgot to send. About a painting that sold for more than yours at last month's show. About whether your gallery is losing interest. About a comment someone made in a workshop six weeks ago that you still can't shake.

The paint is on your palette. But you are not here.

· · ·

Marcus Aurelius had a phrase for the disciplined mind: the inner citadel. He meant the private fortress of your thoughts, the one place no external force can breach unless you open the gates. You can lose your health, your money, your reputation, even your freedom. But your mind remains your own if you choose to govern it.

For artists, this is not abstract philosophy. It is the most practical skill you can develop.

Every painting begins in the mind before it touches the canvas. The decisions that matter most (what to include, what to leave out, where to place the center of interest, how dark to push the darks, when to stop) are all mental acts. If your mind is cluttered, your painting will be cluttered. If your mind is scattered, your brushwork will wander. If your thinking is muddled by anxiety, comparison, or self-doubt, you will overwork, second-guess, and lose the freshness that makes a painting come alive.

Design gives clarity. But design starts in your head, not on the canvas. Before you can simplify the landscape in front of you, you have to simplify the noise inside you.

This does not mean suppressing your emotions. The Stoics have been badly misread on this point. Marcus was not advocating for numbness. He was advocating for choice: the ability to notice what you're feeling, examine whether it's useful, and decide whether to act on it or let it pass. That is not coldness. That is freedom.

Think about the last time you ruined a painting. Not through lack of skill, but through lack of composure. You got anxious about a passage that wasn't working. Instead of stepping back and thinking clearly about the design, you lunged at it with a loaded brush and made it worse. Then you tried to fix the fix. Then the whole thing tightened up and died.

That is not a painting problem. That is a thinking problem.

The inner citadel, for a painter, means this: before you pick up the brush, settle your mind. Know what you're after. Have a plan, even a rough one. And when the painting starts fighting you (as it will) return to the plan instead of reacting out of panic.

In plein air work, this discipline becomes even more essential. You're working against the clock. The light is moving. People are watching. The wind is tearing at your easel. If you let every external disruption invade your mental workspace, you will produce nothing but frustration on a panel.

Marcus wrote something that painters should tape to the inside of their pochade box: "You have power over your mind, not outside events. Realize this, and you will find strength."

The outside events are real. The bad weather. The painting that's not cooperating. The show rejection letter in your inbox. The fellow artist who seems to sail effortlessly while you grind. None of that is under your control. But the way you respond, the story you tell yourself about what it means, that is entirely yours.

Governing your mind is not a one-time achievement. It is a daily practice, like stretching before a run. You don't master it and move on. You return to it every morning, every session, every time you notice your thoughts drifting toward something that isn't helping you paint.

In the studio, this might look like a quiet ritual before you begin. Two minutes of looking at your subject without touching the brush. A thumbnail sketch to clarify the design. A conscious decision about what the painting is about, its story, before you commit a single stroke.

There is a spiritual dimension here worth naming plainly. The mind is not just a tool for productivity. Attention is not merely a technique. The way we attend to the world is part of the way we honor what has been given. To see clearly is not nothing. To notice deeply is not nothing. A scattered mind wastes the gift. A vain mind distorts it. A hurried mind skims past what should have been honored. But a quieted mind begins to receive before it acts.

That word receive matters. Artists are often tempted to think only in terms of making, pushing, solving, proving, expressing. But before any of that, there is receiving. Receiving the subject. Receiving the light. Receiving the mood of the day. Receiving even the fact that one has been given eyes to see and hands to shape. Some of the best painting begins when the artist stops trying to dominate everything and learns how to pay better attention.

In teaching, governing the mind means arriving at your workshop with a clear head and a generous spirit, regardless of what happened in the parking lot or what's waiting in your email. Your students deserve your full attention. You cannot give it if your mind is elsewhere. An instructor's state of mind enters the room before their words do. A restless teacher creates a restless class. The teacher who governs themselves offers a hidden gift: calm, order, and the quiet demonstration that difficulty can be met without panic.

The inner citadel is not a retreat from the world. It is a stance within it. You are still present, still engaged, still feeling. But you are no longer at the mercy of every stray thought, every comparison, every fear. You are painting from a centered place. And the work shows it.

Then, and only then, pick up the brush.

There is one more thing worth saying about governing the mind. An artist may feel fear and still proceed. May feel envy and refuse comparison. May feel discouragement and still mix the next color. May feel scattered and still gather themself enough to see. That is governance. And it is available not only to the naturally serene, but to the ordinary working artist who chooses again and again to come back.

Some of the strongest painters are not the least emotional. They are the ones who have learned not to let emotion seize the wheel. They feel deeply, but they do not let every passing weather system inside them decide the terms of the work. They return to structure. To observation. To simplicity. To gratitude. To the task. That is not repression. It is stewardship of the gift. And it matters because the artist is not only making objects. The artist is also shaping a life. Every day in the studio teaches something. It teaches how to respond to frustration. How to bear limitation. How to work without guarantees. How to return after failure. The brush reveals the person, yes. But it also forms the person.

• • •

Reflections & Journal Prompts

— *What are the three most common mental distractions that pull me away from focused painting?*

— *When was the last time I ruined a painting through anxiety rather than lack of skill? What would I do differently now?*

— *What is my pre-painting ritual? If I don't have one, what would a useful one look like?*

— *How do I currently handle the moment when a painting starts going wrong? Do I react, or do I respond?*

• • •

My oil painting instructor, Eugene Hall, used to say, *"Some mornings I have to drag my stone-cold corpse to the easel."* He said it the way a man says something he has done a thousand times. Not complaining. Just telling the truth. But when he got there, when he picked up the brush and settled into the work, life met him at that easel. His paintings carried a kind of quiet authority that I have rarely seen matched, even in museums. He governed his mind not by never struggling, but by never letting the struggle keep him from the work.

The strongest paintings are made by painters who govern their minds before they govern their brushes. You cannot control the light, the weather, the market, or the opinions of strangers. But you can control where your attention goes. That is enough. That is everything.

CHAPTER 2
The Work in Front of You

Doing What Is Here to Be Done

There is a painting you need to make today. Not the one you're planning for next month's show, or the one you've been dreaming about since that trip to the coast, or the masterpiece that will finally prove you're the real deal. The one that's here. Now. On your schedule or in your head or on the panel you prepped last night.

The question is whether you'll actually do it.

. . .

Marcus Aurelius returned again and again to a single, stubborn principle: do the work that is in front of you. Not tomorrow's work. Not last year's unfinished projects. The task at hand. He wrote that a person should approach each day's duties the way a surgeon approaches an operation: with all instruments ready, focused entirely on the patient on the table.

Artists have a particular genius for avoiding the work in front of them. We research. We organize the studio. We sharpen pencils. We browse other artists' Instagram feeds, telling ourselves it's study. We wait for inspiration, for the right light, for the right mood, for the magical alignment of conditions that will make starting feel effortless.

It never comes. Or rather, it comes after you start. Inspiration follows action, not the other way around. Marcus knew this. He did not wait to feel like governing. He governed because it was his work.

For painters, the principle is devastatingly simple: go to the easel. Mix paint. Put brush to surface. Begin.

The beginning does not need to be brilliant. It needs to exist. A bad start can be corrected. A painting that was never begun cannot.

There is a particular discipline in plein air painting that enforces this truth. You arrive at the site. The light is doing something beautiful but temporary. You have maybe ninety minutes before it changes completely. There is no time for hesitation. You must choose your composition, block in your values, and commit, all within the first few minutes. The clock is ticking. The work is in front of you. Do it or lose it.

Studio painters face a subtler version of the same challenge. Without the urgency of changing light, it's easy to drift. To fuss with the setup. To repaint a passage that was fine the first time. To start three paintings and finish none. The antidote is the same: decide what the work is, and do it.

Marcus was suspicious of busyness that masquerades as productivity. There is a difference between being busy and being effective. An artist can spend eight hours in the studio and accomplish nothing if those hours are filled with indecision, rearranging, and second-guessing. Another artist can accomplish something real in ninety focused minutes because they walked in with a plan and executed it.

Design gives clarity here too. A strong compositional plan is not just an artistic tool. It's a decision-making tool. When you know the value structure you're after, you stop asking yourself what to do next. The design tells you. Light shape here. Shadow mass there. Transition in between. The painting reveals itself through the structure you chose at the start.

Much artistic misery comes from doing one task while demanding that it perform another. A thumbnail is asked to be a masterpiece. A study is asked to prove worth. A class is asked to solve a decade of uncertainty. A new series is judged by mature standards before it has had time to breathe. No wonder so many artists feel crushed.

Marcus would say, in effect, return to the act itself. If you are drawing, draw. If you are simplifying, simplify. If you are blocking in masses, block in masses. There is dignity in each stage when it is allowed to be itself.

There is something worth noting about the relationship between action and clarity. Most painters think they need to see the whole painting before they can start. They want the composition settled, the palette chosen, the mood determined, all before a single stroke goes down. But clarity often comes through the act of painting itself. You block in a dark shape, and suddenly the light pattern reveals itself. You mix a color that surprises you, and the mood shifts in a direction you hadn't planned. The painting teaches you what it wants to be, but only if you start it.

Marcus wrote about the craftsman who picks up his tools and begins. He does not sit in the workshop theorizing about the chair he will build. He selects the wood. He measures. He cuts. The chair emerges from the doing. Your painting is the same.

For teachers, this principle applies to preparation and presence. The work in front of you at a workshop is not to be impressive. It is to serve the students who showed up. Prepare your demonstration. Know your sequence. Teach what you said you would teach, and do it with full attention.

There is a spiritual note here that belongs naturally. Most meaningful work is received in portions. Rarely all at once. More often in daily measures. This hour. This sketch. This student. This passage of light. This decision. We are often given enough for the work of today, not the whole map. Artists do not always like that. We want the larger assurance. But much of the creative life asks for trust without total visibility. It asks us to be faithful with what is in our hands now. That, too, is a form of stewardship.

Do the work in front of you. Not brilliantly. Not perfectly. Just honestly, with full attention, one mark at a time.

A painting has an order to it, whether the artist respects that order or not. First comes seeing. Then selection. Then organization. Then execution. Then refinement, if refinement is truly needed. Trouble begins when the painter skips ahead mentally and tries to resolve things that do not yet deserve attention. Detail before structure. Texture before value. Finish before foundation. Mood before hierarchy. That is how paintings grow confused.

The same thing happens in the inner life. The artist wants certainty before labor. Recognition before body of work. Voice before mileage. Calm before discipline. But most good things in art come in sequence. You do not leap past the smaller jobs and arrive at depth by wishing hard. You earn it by doing what belongs to the hour you are in.

And there is a hidden gift: gratitude. When artists live too far ahead, the present always feels disappointing. Today's study is too small. Today's painting is too ordinary. Today's progress is too slow. But when the artist returns to the immediate task with honest attention, even modest work regains dignity. The little panel matters. The exercise matters. The day becomes livable again. And a livable day is where a real art life is built.

• • •

Reflections & Journal Prompts

— *What painting or project have I been avoiding? What would it take to start it today?*

— *Am I confusing busyness in the studio with actual productive work?*

— *When I arrive at the easel, do I have a plan, or do I wait for something to happen?*

— *What would change if I treated every painting session like a plein air session, with a clock running?*

• • •

Chuck Close once said, *"Inspiration is for amateurs. The rest of us just show up and get to work."* Close painted enormous portraits, some of them ten feet tall, built mark by mark, grid square by grid square. After a spinal artery collapse left him largely paralyzed, he strapped a brush to his hand and kept going. He did not wait to feel ready. He did the work in front of him. That is not stubbornness. That is the practice.

The work does not wait for you to be ready. It waits for you to begin. Marcus governed an empire one day at a time. You can govern a painting one stroke at a time. Start where you are. Use what you have. Do what is in front of you. That is always enough.

CHAPTER 3
What You Cannot Control

Releasing What Is Not Yours to Hold

You submitted your best painting to a national show. The work was strong, the best thing you'd done in years. You knew the design was solid, the story was clear, the paint handling was fresh. You photographed it carefully, emailed it on time, and waited. The rejection email arrived on a Tuesday. No explanation. No feedback. Just: not selected.

Now what?

. . .

The central teaching of Stoic philosophy is the dichotomy of control: some things are in your power, and some things are not. Your opinions, your choices, your effort, your character: these are yours. Everything else (other people's decisions, the market, the weather, whether a jury sees what you see in a painting) is not.

Marcus Aurelius returned to this principle constantly, because life constantly tested it. He lost children. He was betrayed by trusted advisors. He endured a plague that killed millions. And through it all, he kept asking himself the same question: is this within my control?

For artists, the list of things outside our control is long and humbling. Gallery decisions. Collector taste. Show acceptances and rejections. Whether the outdoor painting session gets rained out. Whether the student grasps the lesson. Whether the painting you love gets ignored at the reception while the one you almost didn't hang gets a ribbon.

The list of things within our control is shorter but far more powerful. How hard we work. How honestly we see. How carefully we design. How bravely we simplify. Whether we show up at the easel tomorrow. Whether we prepare for the workshop. Whether we stay generous when it would be easier to be bitter.

This distinction is not about passivity. It is about accuracy. When you waste energy trying to control what you cannot, you drain the reserves you need for the things you can. An artist who spends their morning anxious about whether the gallery will call has less creative energy for the painting on their easel. An artist who paints their best work, sends it into the world, and then returns to the studio: that artist is free.

In the field, this principle is physical and immediate. You set up to paint a gorgeous sunset. The clouds shift. The color drains out of the sky. What do you do? If you rage against the weather, you paint nothing. If you accept the new condition and find the beauty in it, you might paint something unexpected and true. The obstacle becomes the subject.

This is where acceptance deepens seeing. When you stop insisting that the world arrange itself according to your preferences, you start noticing what is actually there. The overcast sky you didn't want becomes a study in subtle value shifts. The rejected painting becomes a lesson in what the jury couldn't see, or in what you couldn't yet execute. The student who doesn't understand your critique gives you a chance to teach more clearly.

Marcus wrote that we should be like a rocky headland against which the waves crash ceaselessly. It stands firm while the fury of the water settles around it. This is not stubbornness. It is stability. The waves are real. The disappointments are real. But they do not define you. Your response defines you.

In practical terms, this means building your art life around the things you can influence and releasing the rest. You can control the quality of your daily practice. You can control how many paintings you make this year. You can control how you prepare for a show. You can control whether you write a kind note to a fellow artist whose work you admire.

You cannot control whether any of that is rewarded. And if you need the reward to keep going, you will eventually stop. The artist who paints only for recognition is at the mercy of forces as unpredictable as the weather. The artist who paints because it is their work, because the seeing and the making are their own reward, that artist is untouchable.

After submitting a painting to a show or sending images to a gallery, give yourself a defined window to think about it. One day, maybe two. Then close the lid. Return to the studio. Start the next painting. You have done what you can do. The decision belongs to someone else now. Your job is to make the next piece of work as strong as possible, regardless of what happens to the last one.

This is also where faith and art meet for many painters. The belief that your gifts were given to you for a purpose, that the ability to see and respond to beauty is not an accident, can sustain you when the external results do not cooperate. You do not paint because the world rewards you. You paint because you were made to see, and seeing demands a response.

This distinction also helps the artist age more honestly. Some things will change whether we welcome them or not. Speed changes. Energy changes. Seasons of caregiving, illness, grief, or interruption come. This can feel cruel if identity is tied only to ideal output. But the wiser question is not only what has changed. It is what still belongs to me now? Perhaps not the same speed. But still observation. Still judgment. Still design. Still simplification. Still teaching. Still gratitude. Still one more honest painting. That is not a lesser life. It is often a deeper one.

There is a kind of freedom here that many artists never quite claim. It says, in effect, I will not spend myself fighting what I was never given power to rule. I will not abandon my agency just because

I cannot command everything. I will tend what is mine to tend. That is mature strength. It also makes for better art.

Two words have served me well in thinking about this kind of strength: Agency and Ramp. Agency is knowing what you need, what to do, and how to do it. It is not waiting for someone to hand you the answer or the opportunity or the permission. It is the quiet confidence of a painter who can assess the scene, choose the composition, identify the value structure, and begin. Not perfectly. But with enough understanding to move forward under her own power. Agency does not mean you know everything. It means you know enough to act, and you know how to find what you do not yet know.

Ramp is the companion to Agency. Ramp is your ability to get up to speed quickly, to shift from standing still to working, even when conditions are not ideal and you do not feel like starting. In plein air work, Ramp is survival. The light is moving. You cannot spend forty minutes easing into the painting. You must arrive, assess, decide, and commit. But Ramp is more than speed. It is also a mindset of fierce curiosity. Be extremely curious. Ask good questions. Study what you do not understand. Learn from painters who are ahead of you. There is always more to learn, and the willingness to stay in that posture of learning is what keeps an artist moving forward when everything else says slow down or stop. Agency gets you to the easel. Ramp gets you painting before the doubt has time to sit down.

· · ·

Reflections & Journal Prompts

— *What am I currently spending energy trying to control that is genuinely outside my power?*

— *What would my art practice look like if I focused only on what I can influence?*

— *When was the last time a setback taught me something I wouldn't have learned from success?*

— *Can I name one thing I need to release today in order to paint more freely?*

· · ·

"Sometimes the thing you cannot control is the thing that saves the work." During the annual Paint Cedarburg event in Wisconsin, I found a whimsical yellow house on Washington Street that I had to paint. I arrived early, set up behind my car with a clear view across the street, drew the composition, and started the underpainting. Then the sky closed up and the rain came in. I packed everything into the car. It rained the rest of the day. I was disappointed. I had a plan and the weather wrecked it. But the next morning the underpainting had dried completely, and something better became possible. I laid transparent washes of ultramarine blue over the warm underpainting to define the shadows. The temperature contrast was alive in a way it never would have been if I had pushed through in one sitting. The opaque lights came next, then a handful of details, and the painting was finished. It won an award. The weather I could not control gave me the painting I could not have planned. That is not always how it works. But it works often enough to pay attention.

The painter who controls her attention, her effort, and her integrity has everything she needs. The rest, the sales, the shows, the applause, comes and goes like weather. Let it. Your job is to paint well and live honestly. The rest is not yours to carry.

CHAPTER 4
The Weight of Other People's Opinions

Handling Criticism and Praise

Two things happened at the same show. A collector looked at your painting for a long time, then said, "This is extraordinary." You floated for a week. A fellow artist glanced at the same painting and muttered, "The values are off in the sky." You couldn't sleep for three nights.

Both of them saw the same painting. Neither of their opinions changed a single brushstroke.

. . .

Marcus Aurelius had an empire's worth of opinions directed at him every day. Senators praised him. Enemies cursed him. Philosophers debated his policies. Soldiers grumbled. And he kept reminding himself: their opinions are their own affair. What matters is whether I am doing the right thing.

Artists live in a world saturated with opinions, some invited, most not. Social media has made every painting a public referendum the moment it's posted. Likes, comments, silence. Each one lands somewhere in the nervous system and does its work. We say we don't care about the numbers. We check them anyway.

The stoic position is not to be indifferent to all feedback. It is to be intelligent about which feedback deserves your attention and how much weight to give it.

There are three categories of opinion that matter in an artist's life. The first is expert critique: feedback from someone who knows more than you about the specific skill in question. If a master painter tells you your values are too close in the shadow, that is information worth receiving with humility and attention. The second is honest response: the reaction of a thoughtful viewer who may not know the technical language but feels something real in front of the painting. That is also worth receiving, because paintings are made for human beings, not for technicians. The third is noise: everything else. The anonymous comment. The casual dismissal at a reception. The compliment that's really about the commenter. The criticism that's really about the critic's own frustration.

The discipline is in sorting these quickly and acting only on what is useful.

Praise is its own danger. Marcus warned against becoming addicted to approval, because it turns you into a performer. The painter who chases likes begins to paint for likes. The painter who needs the gallery's enthusiasm begins to paint what the gallery wants. Slowly, the work loses its honesty. The freshness drains out because the artist is no longer painting what they see. They are painting what they think will be applauded.

This happens quietly. A certain palette gets compliments, so it becomes a formula. A certain subject sells, so it becomes a habit. A certain kind of loose brushwork gets admired, so looseness becomes affectation. A social media post does well, so the artist starts feeding the machine instead of feeding the work. None of this begins with bad intent. It begins with wanting to be received. That is human. But once that becomes the ruling desire, the work starts bending away from truth.

Criticism, handled well, is one of the most powerful accelerants in an artist's development. Handled poorly, it is poison. The key is to separate the information from the emotion. If someone tells you the foreground is competing with the focal point, that is a design observation you can evaluate on its own merits. You don't have to like the way it was delivered. You just have to ask: is it true?

In the teaching studio, this cuts both ways. As an instructor, your critiques carry weight. A careless remark can shut a student down for months. A well-placed, specific observation can unlock years of progress. The stoic approach to giving critique is the same as receiving it: be honest, be specific, be kind, and aim at what is useful rather than what is impressive.

Design, Story, Freshness provides a framework for critique that is honest without being cruel. Does the design work? Is there a clear value plan and a visual path? Does the painting tell a story, does it communicate feeling, place, light, or mood? And does it feel fresh, does it show the mark of a painter who was present and confident, not labored and frightened? Those three questions will serve you better than any amount of vague encouragement or vague complaint.

There is one more form of opinion that deserves attention: the opinion of the market. Sales are a kind of feedback, and they can be seductive. When a particular subject or style sells well, the temptation is to keep repeating it. And while there is nothing wrong with painting what people want to buy, there is a danger in letting the market become your only compass. The market rewards what is familiar. Your growth as an artist requires that you attempt what is unfamiliar. These two forces are in constant tension.

Paint some work for the market. Paint some work for yourself. Keep both streams flowing. The market work pays the bills. The personal work feeds the soul. Marcus would understand this balance. He governed an empire, which required constant compromise and pragmatism. But he kept his private journal, which was pure and uncompromised. The public work and the private work served different masters, and he did not confuse them.

Guard your inner compass. Let it be informed by honest critique and genuine response. Let it be sharpened by expert feedback. But do not surrender it to the noise.

There is another layer here. Applause can become addictive not only publicly but privately. An artist may begin chasing their own self-congratulation. They want to feel impressive, profound, original, important. That appetite can distort the work just as surely as outside praise. It produces paintings that strain to be significant rather than becoming so through honesty, restraint, and form.

Marcus helps cut through this. He repeatedly humbles the self, not to shame it, but to put it in proper scale. We are temporary. So are our admirers. So are our critics. So are most reputations. What remains is the quality of the work, the quality of character, and the quality of one's use of time. That is a healthier standard. The artist who learns this becomes freer. Not numb. Not aloof. But less easily rattled. Praise no longer intoxicates so easily. Criticism no longer wounds so deeply. The work can be done with a steadier pulse. And a steadier pulse usually makes better art.

• • •

Reflections & Journal Prompts

— *Whose critical feedback do I actually trust? Why?*

— *Am I currently painting toward approval rather than toward truth?*

— *When I give a critique, do I aim for what is useful or what makes me sound knowledgeable?*

— *What is the most valuable piece of criticism I have ever received, and what made me able to hear it?*

• • •

Georgia O'Keeffe once wrote in a letter, *"I have already settled it for myself so flattery and criticism go down the same drain and I am quite free."* She painted bones in the desert while the art world chased abstraction in New York. She painted flowers so large that people had to stop and actually see them. She did not paint for the critics. She did not paint against them. She painted what was hers to paint, and she let the opinions fall where they fell. That kind of freedom is not indifference. It is clarity about where your compass points.

The opinion that matters most is the one you hold after a long, honest look at your own work with clear eyes and a quiet mind. Other voices can sharpen that vision. They should never replace it.

CHAPTER 5
The Ego Trap

Humility and the Danger of Self-Importance

You finish a painting that sings. The color is alive. The edges are varied and purposeful. The whole thing breathes. You step back and feel a flush of something warm and dangerous: the thought that you have arrived. That you are, finally, as good as you always suspected.

Enjoy it for exactly five minutes. Then put it away.

· · ·

Marcus Aurelius governed the most powerful empire on earth, and he spent a surprising amount of his private journal reminding himself that he was not special. He wrote about the brevity of fame, the sameness of all human striving, the fact that emperors before him had been forgotten as thoroughly as the servants who cleaned their floors. This was not self-hatred. It was perspective.

Ego is the artist's most seductive enemy, because it disguises itself as confidence. Confidence says: I can handle this. I've done the work. I trust my eye. Ego says: I am better than them. I deserve more than I'm getting. My work should be recognized. The difference matters enormously, because confidence makes you brave and ego makes you brittle.

Ego in art is rarely as obvious as people imagine. It does not always look like swagger or boasting. Often it arrives dressed in more respectable clothes. It can look like perfectionism. Like oversensitivity. Like needing to be original at all costs. Like refusing help. Like taking every setback personally. Like quietly believing one is either above correction or beneath hope. Ego does not only swell. It also bruises.

In the studio, ego shows up in subtle ways. It tells you to keep adding to a painting that is already finished, because more work means more proof of your skill. It tells you not to try a new approach because you might look foolish. It tells you that your way of painting is the right way and that other approaches are lesser. It makes you competitive when you should be curious.

In teaching, ego is toxic. The instructor whose ego is invested in being the smartest person in the room will teach defensively, protecting his authority rather than serving his students. He will dismiss questions that challenge his methods. He will demonstrate to impress rather than to instruct. And the students will learn less, because learning requires openness, and openness cannot survive in the presence of someone else's need to be right.

Marcus credited his teachers by name at the beginning of Meditations. He listed what each one taught him, not to impress, but to remember. This is the posture of a lifelong student, and it is the healthiest posture an artist can take.

The best painters I know remain students their entire careers. They study other artists with genuine admiration. They take workshops, even after decades of experience. They walk into a museum and let themselves be humbled by work that surpasses their own. This is not weakness. It is the engine of growth.

Ego also distorts the way we see our own work. The ego-driven painter cannot evaluate his paintings honestly, because honesty might reveal something unflattering. He explains away weaknesses. He blames the jury, the gallery, the public. Meanwhile, the humble painter looks at her painting and says, "The design is strong, but the color in the middle ground is dead. I'll fix that next time." She is free to improve because she is not defending a false image of herself.

Story is the antidote to ego. When the painting is about the story (about the light falling through the trees, about the mood of the harbor at dusk, about the quiet dignity of a face) it takes the artist out of the center. The painting serves something larger than the painter. And paradoxically, that is when the painter's best, most authentic self comes through.

Comparison is ego's favorite tool. When you look at another artist's work and feel that sour twist in your stomach, that mixture of admiration and resentment, that is ego talking. The stoic response is not to suppress the feeling but to redirect it. What, specifically, is that artist doing well? Can you learn from it? Can you admire it without needing to compete with it? Admiration without envy is one of the highest skills an artist can develop. Marcus practiced it with his teachers. You can practice it with your peers.

A practical guard against ego is to keep a "failure file": a stack of paintings that did not work. Not to punish yourself, but to stay honest. Look at them periodically. They are proof that you are human, that you are still learning, and that every painting is a risk.

One sign that ego has entered the room is when curiosity leaves. Ego already knows. Ego poses. Ego defends. Ego compares. Humility asks better questions. What does this need? What am I missing? What would make this clearer? Curiosity keeps the work alive. Ego often stiffens it.

Marcus wrote that we should work like a vine that produces grapes, without expecting anything in return. The vine does not demand applause for its fruit. It simply does what it was made to do. There is something deeply peaceful about approaching your art life this way. You make the work. You make it as well as you can. You let it go. And then you make the next one.

• • •

Reflections & Journal Prompts

— *Where is ego currently distorting my view of my own work?*

— *Am I still a student? When was the last time I let myself be genuinely taught?*

— *Do I paint to express something true or to prove something about myself?*

— *What would my art life look like if I never needed anyone to
be impressed?*

• • •

Edgar Degas put it simply: *"Painting is easy when you don't know
how, but very difficult when you do."* The beginner thinks he is close
to mastery because he does not yet know how far away it is. The experienced painter knows exactly how far, and that knowledge is both
humbling and useful. Ego shrinks in the presence of real understanding. The more honestly you see what the work demands, the less room
there is for posturing.

**Ego promises significance and delivers fragility. Humility
promises nothing and delivers freedom. The best artists make
the best work not because they think they are great, but because they forget themselves long enough to see clearly.**

CHAPTER 6
The Discipline of Returning

Consistency, Rhythm, and the Long Practice

The painter who works every day is not always inspired. Some mornings the colors look dull. The subject doesn't excite them. The brush feels clumsy. They paint anyway.

After thirty years, they have a body of work that fills a room. The painter who works only when inspiration strikes has a handful of promising starts.

. . .

Marcus Aurelius woke up every morning and did his job. He did not always want to. In one of the most honest passages in Meditations, he wrote about the temptation to stay in bed: the warmth of the covers, the appeal of doing nothing. And then he told himself: you were not made for comfort. You were made for work. Get up.

This is not glamorous advice. It will never go viral. But it is the single most important habit a serious artist can develop: the discipline of returning to the work, day after day, whether you feel like it or not.

Inspiration is wonderful when it arrives. It gives you energy, clarity, speed. But it is unreliable. It comes and goes like good light on a cloudy day. If you wait for it, you will produce very little. If you work without it, you will often find that it shows up mid-session, drawn by the act of working itself.

There is a mechanical truth underneath this: skill lives in your hands, and hands need repetition. A painter who works daily develops a physical fluency that a painter who works sporadically cannot match. The brush knows what to do because it has done it a thousand times before. Edges become intuitive. Mixing becomes automatic.

The gap between seeing and executing narrows. And that gap is where freshness lives, in the speed and confidence of a painter who trusts the process enough to let the paint breathe.

Rhythm may be the better word for what artists need. Rhythm suggests recurrence. Cadence. Breathing. A pattern of return that carries the body and mind back to the work without excessive drama.

Patience is the companion of consistency. Marcus wrote about endurance not as suffering but as a form of staying power. The long career, the slow accumulation of skill, the gradual deepening of vision: none of these happen in a burst. They happen over years of steady, undramatic effort.

This is hard for artists in a culture that celebrates breakthroughs, overnight discoveries, and the myth of natural genius. The truth is less exciting and more durable: most great painters became great through sustained, patient practice. They painted hundreds of paintings no one will ever see. They worked through bad periods. They kept going when the results didn't match their ambition.

For teachers, the discipline of returning applies to pedagogy as well. Good teaching requires repetition. You will explain value structure for the two hundredth time to a new class of beginners, and you must do it with the same care and energy as the first time. This is not tedious if you understand it correctly: each student is hearing it for the first time. Your job is to make it alive for them.

The practical shape of this discipline is simple. Set a schedule. Protect it. Paint three days a week, or five, or every day, whatever is sustainable for your life. The number matters less than the regularity. An artist who paints three hours every Tuesday and Thursday will outpace an artist who paints ten-hour bursts every three weeks.

Keep a painting log. Record what you worked on, what went well, what didn't. This is your own version of Meditations: a journal for the working artist. Over time, patterns emerge. You start to see where you consistently struggle, where you consistently succeed, and where the next level of growth is waiting.

Here is a truth that experienced painters know but rarely say aloud: the paintings you make when you do not feel like painting are often among your best. Why? Because the ego is quiet. The expectations are low. You are not trying to make a masterpiece; you are just trying to get through the session. And in that stripped-down state, something honest happens. The brushwork loosens. The decisions become intuitive rather than strategic. The freshness that you chase on your best days shows up uninvited on the days you almost didn't bother.

This is not mystical. It is mechanical. When you are relaxed and expectations are low, your body does what it has been trained to do. Muscle memory takes over. The analytical mind, which so often interferes with fluid painting, steps aside because it has nothing to prove.

There is a spiritual note here that belongs near the center. Rhythm is not only about efficiency. It is about faithfulness. The return to the easel, the sketchbook, the walk, the lesson plan, the value study: these are not merely acts of productivity. They can become acts of stewardship. Small acts of obedience. A way of saying, "This gift will not be neglected simply because today I feel dull, distracted, or discouraged."

Do not romanticize the struggle. Just do the work. Marcus didn't need motivation speeches. He needed his own willingness to get up and face the day. So do you.

There is also freedom in rhythm. Decision fatigue lessens. The artist no longer negotiates every day from scratch. There is a known path back. A table. A chair. A sketchbook. A walk. A time of day. A first exercise. The start becomes less dramatic, and because it is less dramatic, it becomes easier. Many artists do not lack desire. They lack reentry. They do not know how to get back in once life has crowded the edges of the work. Rhythm solves this by building a ramp rather than demanding a leap.

Rhythm also helps artists endure dry seasons. Not every season will feel fertile. Some weeks the work will be mechanical. Some months the paintings will disappoint. The artist without rhythm often interprets these seasons as identity statements: I've lost it. Maybe I'm done. But the artist with rhythm is less likely to panic. They know dryness is part of the weather, not the whole climate. They keep the door open. A quick sketch. A value study. A walk with a notebook. Not every return must be grand to remain faithful.

One of the hidden graces of rhythm is that it slowly forms trust. Not trust in constant success, but trust that return matters. Trust that one imperfect session does not end the path. Trust that small daily faithfulness accumulates even when visible progress feels thin. Trust that the gift grows by being used, not merely admired from a distance.

· · ·

Reflections & Journal Prompts

— *What is my current painting schedule? Is it consistent, or does it depend on mood?*

— *If I committed to painting at the same time on the same days each week, what would need to change?*

— *Do I keep a record of my painting sessions? What might I learn from one?*

— *What is the longest dry spell I've had, and what pulled me out of it?*

· · ·

Vincent van Gogh wrote to his brother Theo, *"If you hear a voice within you say 'you cannot paint,' then by all means paint, and that voice will be silenced."* Van Gogh knew that voice well. He heard it most of his life. He painted anyway. Not because he had conquered the doubt, but because he refused to let the doubt make the decision. The voice does not go away. You simply learn to pick up the brush while it is still talking.

The brush does not care whether you feel inspired. It cares whether you pick it up. Return to the work. Return again. Return until returning is no longer a decision but a reflex, as natural as breathing, as steady as the tide.

CHAPTER 7
Simplify Everything

The Power of Leaving Things Out

You are painting a woodland stream. There are rocks, moss, re-flections, fallen branches, ferns, dappled light, and the dark shapes of hemlocks behind it all. You can see everything. The question is: should you paint everything?

No. The answer is almost always no.

· · ·

Marcus Aurelius prized simplicity as a moral virtue. He wrote about stripping away the unnecessary, in thought, in speech, in action. He distrusted complexity for its own sake. He believed that most problems became manageable once you removed the layers of drama, speculation, and self-importance that people draped over them.

For painters, this translates into one of the most powerful principles in the craft: the strength of what you leave out.

A painting is not a photograph. It is not an inventory of everything visible in the scene. It is a designed arrangement of shapes, values, and colors organized to tell a story. Every element either serves that design and that story, or it competes with it. There is no neutral. Everything in the painting is either working for you or against you.

This is where Design gives clarity becomes more than a nice phrase. A clear value plan, a strong pattern of light and shadow, requires the painter to make ruthless choices. That stand of trees on the left? It breaks the light pattern. Lose it. The fence posts in the middle ground? They create competing verticals. Simplify them or remove them. The third boat in the harbor? Two tell the story. Three clutter it.

Beginning painters add. Experienced painters subtract. The journey from one to the other is the journey from recording to designing, from copying to interpreting, from showing everything to saying something.

Marcus wrote about the beauty of plainness: the crack in a loaf of bread, the way olives look just before they become overripe. He saw beauty in simplicity because he trained himself to look at what was essential rather than what was decorative. Painters who learn to do this make stronger work.

Simplicity also applies to your palette. You do not need forty colors to paint the world. A limited palette, three or four colors plus white, forces you to mix with intention. It creates harmony automatically because every mixture shares the same parent colors. It prevents the scattered, disconnected look that comes from reaching for a new tube every time you need a note.

In brushwork, simplicity means confidence. One stroke that says what it means is worth ten hesitant ones. Fresh, direct painting comes from knowing what you want to say and saying it without apology. Overworking is almost always a symptom of not having simplified the problem enough before you started painting.

For teachers, the principle of simplification is essential. When you teach, you must distill complex visual problems into simple, actionable steps. "Squint and find the big shapes" is better instruction than a twenty-minute lecture on visual perception. "Get your darks right first" is better than a color theory seminar. Students need handles they can grab. Give them three things, not thirty.

Constraints breed creativity. A time limit forces decisions. A small canvas demands economy. A limited palette demands ingenuity. These are not obstacles. They are allies. Marcus understood this about life: the fewer things you chase, the more fully you can pursue the ones that matter.

There is a useful exercise: paint the same subject three times. The first time, include everything you see. The second time, remove a third of the elements. The third time, reduce the painting to its absolute essentials: the fewest shapes, the simplest value plan, the minimum information needed to tell the story. Compare the three. Nearly always, the third version is the strongest. Not because it is empty, but because everything in it is necessary.

Marcus wrote about a figure who could say in ten words what others needed a hundred to express. The same economy applies to paint. The masters you admire, the painters whose work stops you in a gallery, are not showing you everything they can do. They are showing you only what the painting needs. The rest they leave out, and that restraint is what gives the work its authority.

Simplicity in your art life extends beyond the canvas. How many social media platforms do you maintain? How many organizations do you belong to? How many commitments fill your calendar that have nothing to do with making or teaching art? Marcus would ask: which of these are essential, and which are just habit? The hours you spend on the inessential are hours stolen from the easel. Guard them.

Simplify your studio setup. Simplify your palette. Simplify your design. Simplify the story you're telling. And then paint with the freedom that comes from knowing exactly what you're after.

. . .

Reflections & Journal Prompts

— *What is one thing I routinely include in my paintings that doesn't serve the design or story?*

— *Could I paint my next piece with three colors and white? What would that force me to learn?*

— *When I teach, do I give students three clear priorities or overwhelm them with complexity?*

— *Where in my art life am I holding onto things that could be simplified or released?*

. . .

Hans Hofmann taught generations of painters one core truth: *"The ability to simplify means to eliminate the unnecessary so that the necessary may speak."* Hofmann understood that a painting does not get stronger by adding more. It gets stronger when the artist has the nerve to strip it down to what actually matters. Every shape that does not serve the design dilutes it. Every detail that does not support the story competes with it. Simplification is not timidity. It is the most confident decision a painter can make.

Simplicity is not laziness. It is the hard-won clarity that comes from knowing what matters and having the courage to let go of everything else. The painter who can say it in five strokes has more authority than the one who says it in fifty.

CHAPTER 8
The Obstacle as Material

Using Difficulty as Creative Fuel

Rain on painting day. A failed demonstration in front of forty students. A canvas that cracked in transit. A hand injury that won't heal. A year when nothing sold.

These are not interruptions to your art life. They are your art life.

. . .

Marcus Aurelius wrote that the impediment to action advances action, that what stands in the way becomes the way. This is one of the most counterintuitive and powerful ideas in all of Stoicism, and it has direct, daily application for artists.

Every serious painter has a catalog of failures. Paintings that went wrong in public. Demos that fell apart. Rejections that stung. Periods of creative drought so long they felt permanent. These experiences are universal. What separates the artists who endure from those who quit is not talent. It is the willingness to use the difficulty rather than be defeated by it.

A failed painting is data. If you can look at it with clear eyes, not defensive eyes, not despairing eyes, but the honest eyes of someone who wants to learn, it will tell you exactly where your understanding broke down. Was it the value structure? The drawing? The color temperature? The composition? Each failed painting points to the next lesson. If you are willing to read it, failure is the most efficient teacher you will ever have.

Physical limitations become creative constraints, and creative constraints produce innovation. The painter with a sore wrist learns to work with larger brushes and fewer strokes, and discovers a boldness she didn't know she had. The painter who can't afford exotic pigments learns to do extraordinary things with a limited palette. The plein air painter caught in unexpected weather abandons the sunny composition she planned and paints the gray mood instead, finding something more interesting than what she came for.

Marcus wrote that fire turns everything thrown into it into fuel. Obstacles are fuel if you choose to treat them that way.

This does not mean pretending that difficulty is pleasant. It means refusing to be stopped by it. There is a difference between denial and resilience. Denial says the problem doesn't exist. Resilience says the problem is real, and I am going to work with it rather than against it.

In teaching, this principle is especially important. The workshop where everything goes smoothly is easy. The workshop where the demo falls apart, that is where real teaching happens. The instructor who can say, "Well, this isn't working. Let me show you why, and let me show you what I'd do to recover," teaches more in that moment than in three perfect demonstrations. Because students are going to fail. Constantly. And what they need most is to see a trusted painter handle failure with honesty and composure.

The obstacle is material in another sense too. The gnarled tree, the muddy road, the overcast sky, the ruined building: the things that are not conventionally beautiful often make the most compelling paintings. Marcus found beauty in imperfection. Painters do too, when they stop insisting that the world look the way they planned.

Consider how many of the most celebrated paintings in history came from difficulty. The Impressionists were rejected by the Salon and painted outdoors out of defiance, which led to an entirely new way of seeing light. Monet painted his water lilies while his eyesight was failing, and the late paintings are among the most profound things in the history of art. The obstacle did not stop the work. It became the work. But you do not need to be Monet to experience this. It happens in ordinary studios and ordinary workshops every week.

I use a story in my workshops that surprises people every time. Imagine an open lot next to a school. No fence. No boundary. Just grass running right to the street. At recess, the children play carefully in the center of that lot. They hold back. They watch the edges. They are free in theory but cautious in practice, because the openness itself feels dangerous.

Now put a fence around that lot. The same children play with their whole bodies. They run to every corner. They use the entire space. They are louder, braver, more alive. The fence did not shrink their world. It freed them to use all of it.

That is exactly what happens in the studio. Most artists walk in with unlimited time, unlimited colors, and unlimited brushstrokes. And at the end of the day they come out with less than they expected. Everything was available, so nothing forced a decision. But hand me thirty minutes and a limited palette and tell me to make a quick study, and the result is almost always fresher, bolder, and more alive than the painting I labored over all afternoon.

This is the irony of creative work. Barriers do not limit freedom. They create it. A time limit forces you to commit. A limited palette forces you to mix with intention. A small canvas forces you to simplify. Even limiting your brushstrokes forces every mark to carry more weight. Your brain treats each constraint as a problem to solve, and in solving it, you make decisions you never would have made with all the room in the world. The freshness that comes from working within real limits is something you simply cannot get any other way. The fence is not the enemy of play. It is what makes the whole playground available.

There is a line worth drawing here between real obstacles and self-made chaos. Poor preparation is not a spiritual discipline. Sloppiness is not a teacher. We should not glorify avoidable trouble. Marcus would have no patience for self-inflicted confusion masquerading as noble struggle. So ask plainly: is this a real limitation, or am I meeting the consequences of my own carelessness?

But where the obstacle is real and unavoidable, the artist has a choice. Resist reality and lose strength. Or meet reality, learn from it, and perhaps become larger inside than before.

In the field, this attitude transforms the painting day. The fog that obscured your planned vista becomes a study in soft edges and close values. The construction site that ruined the foreground becomes an exercise in creative cropping. The wind that won't stop shaking your easel becomes a reason to paint smaller and faster. Each limitation forces a creative decision that would not have existed without the obstacle. And creative decisions, made under pressure, are where fresh painting lives.

· · ·

Reflections & Journal Prompts

— *What is my most recent painting failure, and what did it teach me?*

— *Is there a physical or logistical limitation in my current practice that could become a creative advantage?*

— *How do I currently respond when a demo or painting session goes wrong in front of others?*

— *What is the best painting I ever made that started as a mistake?*

— *What constraint could I impose on my next painting session (time, palette, brush count, canvas size) that might force better decisions?*

· · ·

Near the end of his life, Pierre-Auguste Renoir suffered from rheumatoid arthritis so severe that brushes had to be strapped to his crippled hands. When asked why he kept painting in such pain, he answered, *"The pain passes, but the beauty remains."* He did not stop. He adapted. His late work is looser, warmer, and more luminous than anything he painted with healthy hands. The limitation did not end his art. It changed it into something he could not have reached without the suffering. That is the obstacle becoming the material.

The oak tree does not grow straight because it encountered no wind. It grows strong because the wind forced it to build deeper roots. Your obstacles are building your art in ways you cannot see yet. Keep working. The resistance is the gift.

CHAPTER 9
The Brevity of All Things

Mortality, Time, and Work That Matters

You will not paint forever. The hands will slow. The eyes will change. The mornings at the easel will eventually end. This is not morbid. It is clarifying.

What would you paint today if you understood this, really understood it?

· · ·

Marcus Aurelius thought about death more than most people are comfortable with. But he did not think about it to be gloomy. He thought about it to be awake. The awareness of death, for Marcus, was the ultimate priority-setting tool. If you know your time is limited, you stop wasting it on things that do not matter.

Artists waste time in predictable ways. We procrastinate on the paintings we most want to make, telling ourselves we are not ready yet. We spend years developing skills we never deploy because we are afraid of falling short of our own ambitions. We paint safe subjects because risky ones might fail. We put off the big project, the personal project, the one that would really say something, and we fill our time with small, comfortable work that does not require us to be brave.

Marcus would ask: how long do you plan to wait?

The brevity of time is not just about mortality in the literal sense, though that is real enough. It is about the finite nature of every moment, including the moment at the easel. Plein air painters know this viscerally. The light will not hold. The colors are changing. The subject you love right now will be gone in an hour. This urgency produces some of the most alive painting in the history of the medium. Why?

Because the painter knows she cannot afford to waste a stroke.

Studio painters need to import this urgency. Not as panic, but as focus. Treat every session as if the light is moving, even when it isn't. Make decisions. Commit to them. Don't hedge. The painting is finite. Your energy is finite. Your career is finite. Use them.

This awareness changes what you choose to paint. When time feels limitless, you paint whatever comes along. When you understand that time is short, you start asking better questions. What do I actually want to say? What subjects move me most deeply? What am I afraid to attempt? What would I regret not painting?

Story takes on weight here. A painting that tells a true story, that captures something the painter genuinely cared about, carries a different energy than a painting made to fill a slot in a show. Viewers can feel it. The difference between a painting that was made because the artist had to make it and a painting that was made because the artist needed inventory: that difference is felt even by people who cannot name it.

As artists age, many discover that they no longer want merely attractive scenes. They want resonance. They want work that carries memory, endurance, recovery, stillness, mercy, warmth in cold places, light in darkness, or the quiet dignity of ordinary life. They want the work to say something truer than "I can paint." They want it to answer life more deeply. That shift is usually healthy. It means the artist is no longer content merely to perform skill.

Marcus also thought about legacy, though he was skeptical of fame. He knew that emperors were forgotten. He knew that statues crumble. And yet he still did the work, not for the memory, but because doing good work well was its own justification.

Legacy does not have to mean fame, museums, or a grand cultural footprint. It may include the body of work you leave behind, yes. But it may also mean the students you helped, the courage you stirred, the beauty you returned to the world, the language you gave others, the example of steadiness you embodied, the truth you served in your corner of things. That is not small.

Many artists would live more sanely if they adopted a humbler, richer idea of legacy. Not, "Will I be remembered by many?" but, "Did I spend my life on work worth doing?" Not, "Did I get enough attention?" but, "Did I answer faithfully to what I had been given?" Those questions purify ambition without killing it.

Time also forces practical clarity. It is easier to say no when time is seen clearly. Easier to stop chasing every invitation. Easier to trim platforms that drain life. Easier to focus on the subjects, teachings, and relationships that actually belong to the arc of your work. Easier to choose depth over sprawl.

If design gives clarity, spend time studying design. If story gives meaning, spend time looking for meaning, not just scenery. If freshness gives life, spend time building courage, limits, and decisiveness rather than endless correction. Time tells the truth about priorities more clearly than speech.

In the studio, this becomes practical very fast. Paint the subject that truly holds you, not the one you think you ought to paint. Return to first principles rather than endlessly circling secondary issues. Start the series you keep postponing. Finish the work that deserves finishing. Abandon what no longer belongs to your real direction. Give yourself fewer projects and fuller presence.

Paint what matters to you. Paint it now. Do not wait for conditions to be perfect. They will never be perfect. The light is moving. It is always moving.

• • •

Reflections & Journal Prompts

— *What painting have I been postponing because I am afraid it won't be good enough?*

— *If I could only paint ten more paintings in my lifetime, what would they be?*

— *Am I spending my painting time on work that matters to me, or on work that seems safe?*

— *What do I want my creative legacy to be, not in fame, but in substance?*

• • •

Claude Monet once said, *"I would like to paint the way a bird sings."* Not for an audience. Not for a legacy. Not to prove anything. Just because the song is there and the morning is short and the impulse to respond to beauty is stronger than the impulse to explain it. That is what urgency looks like when it is clean. Not panic. Not ambition. Just a painter who knows the light will not wait, and neither should he.

You were given a set of eyes, a set of hands, and an unknown number of days. Use them. Paint the painting that scares you. Paint the one you have been saving for when you are ready. You are ready enough. The light is moving.

CHAPTER 10
Teaching as Practice

Service, Generosity, and the Art of Passing It On

You are standing at the front of a room. Twelve painters are watching you. They have paid money and driven hours and trusted you with a weekend of their creative lives.

This is not about you.

. . .

Marcus Aurelius opened his Meditations by naming the people who taught him and listing, specifically, what each one gave him. From his grandfather: character and self-control. From his mother: simplicity and generosity. The first act of his private journal was gratitude for his teachers.

If you teach, you hold a position of real influence. A single well-timed observation can change the way a student sees for the rest of her life. A single dismissive remark can close a door that takes years to reopen. Teaching is not a side hustle. It is a responsibility.

The stoic approach to teaching starts with a shift in orientation: from performance to service. You are not demonstrating to impress. You are demonstrating to instruct. The difference is visible. An instructor who paints to impress uses techniques designed to dazzle: big confident strokes that work because of forty years of practice, without explaining the underlying decisions that make those strokes possible. An instructor who paints to instruct slows down enough to narrate the thinking. She explains why she is squinting. She describes what she is looking for in the value structure. She names the choice she is making and the alternatives she rejected.

This is harder than performing. It requires you to disassemble your own intuition and lay the parts on the table. But it is the only way students actually learn.

In performance-driven teaching, the demo becomes harder to imitate because it is too wrapped in personality. The explanations become too many because the teacher is enjoying their own fluency. The critique becomes too broad because the teacher wants to say everything they know. The room begins to admire rather than practice. Students feel the gap between the teacher's ease and their own confusion. Service teaches differently. The service-minded teacher simplifies. They diagnose rather than display. They speak to what matters now.

Marcus believed that human beings are made for each other, that we are social creatures whose highest function is to serve the whole. For artists, this means that the gifts you've been given, your eye, your skill, your understanding of light and form, are not just for you. They are meant to be passed along.

Teaching deepens your own practice in ways that solitary studio work cannot. When you have to explain why a value grouping works, you understand it more thoroughly yourself. When a student asks a question you've never considered, you are forced to think more precisely about something you've been doing on instinct. Teaching keeps your fundamentals sharp because you are constantly returning to first principles.

Short, focused demonstrations, repeated several times throughout a workshop, are more effective than single long ones. Students learn by seeing the process multiple times and then immediately applying it. Give them three priorities, not thirty. Set them up to succeed quickly and build confidence through repetition.

The best critique follows the same framework: name what is working, name what is not, and offer the single change that would help most. Use Design, Story, and Freshness as the lens. Is the design clear? Does the painting communicate a story? Does it feel fresh and alive? If you can answer those three questions honestly and specifically, you have given the student a compass, not just a correction.

Generosity in teaching also means being honest about what you don't know. Marcus admired teachers who did not pretend to have answers they lacked. Saying "I'm not sure, but here's how I'd think about it" is more useful than faking expertise. It also models the intellectual honesty that every serious artist needs.

There is a particular kind of teaching moment that only happens when the instructor is vulnerable. It comes when you stand in front of a class and say, "I don't know why this passage isn't working. Let me think about it out loud." In that moment, you are modeling the most important skill in painting: the ability to look honestly at something that is not working and think through the problem instead of panicking. Your students will remember that moment longer than any dazzling brushstroke.

If you have knowledge, share it. If you have experience, offer it. If you have made mistakes, describe them. The art world is not a zero-sum game. Another painter's growth does not diminish your own. Marcus believed that human beings thrive when they serve each other. The teaching studio, at its best, is one of the clearest expressions of that principle.

Your students are watching how you handle difficulty, how you respond to your own mistakes, how you talk about your own work. They are learning not just your technique but your posture, your relationship to the creative life. If that posture is generous, honest, and disciplined, you are teaching something more valuable than brushwork. You are teaching a way of being an artist.

• • •

Reflections & Journal Prompts

— *When I teach, am I performing or serving? How can I tell the difference?*

— *Who were my most important teachers, and what specifically did each one give me?*
— *In my last critique, did I give the student the one thing that would help most, or did I give them everything I noticed?*
— *How does teaching change my own understanding of the work?*

· · ·

Robert Henri, one of the great teachers in the history of American painting, once told his students, *"Don't take me as an authority. I am simply expressing a very personal point of view. Nothing final about it. You have to find your own way."* Henri could have played the master. He had the skill, the reputation, and the classroom presence to dominate any room. Instead he opened the door and stepped aside. That is what teaching looks like when it is service rather than performance. You hand the student the compass. Then you trust them to walk.

The teacher who gives freely receives more than he spends. Marcus knew this. The wisdom you hand to another painter does not leave your hands. It deepens there. Teach with generosity. The gift returns tenfold.

CHAPTER 11
The Dry Season

Enduring When Nothing Works

There will come a stretch, weeks, maybe months, when the paintings don't come together. The colors will be wrong. The compositions will feel forced. You will stand in front of the easel and feel nothing but blankness where the seeing used to be.

This is normal. It is not the end. It is winter.

. . .

Marcus Aurelius endured a plague that ravaged the empire for years. He lost soldiers, administrators, friends. The economy contracted. The borders were under constant pressure. And he kept working. Not because things were going well, but because working was what was required.

Every serious artist hits dry seasons. They come without warning and they do not announce their departure. The paintings that were flowing suddenly stop. The confidence that felt natural yesterday evaporates. You look at your recent work and see nothing but mediocrity. You look at other artists' work and see nothing but brilliance.

The Stoics had a word for endurance under difficulty: they called it fortitude. Not grim, teeth-clenching endurance, but a steady willingness to keep moving forward without demanding that the universe cooperate. Marcus distinguished between wanting things to be different and being willing to work with things as they are. In a dry season, the artist who demands that inspiration return is miserable. The artist who accepts the drought and keeps painting anyway is building something even though she cannot see it yet.

What happens during a dry season? Often, more than you think.

Your skills are being tested at a deeper level. The crutch of easy success is gone, and you are forced to rely on fundamentals: design, value structure, the mechanics of seeing. This is unglamorous work, but it is strengthening work. When the dry season ends (and it will) you will paint with a solidity you did not have before.

There are practical things you can do to survive a drought. Go back to basics. Paint small studies with no ambition attached. Do value sketches in a notebook. Copy a painting you admire, not to steal but to understand. Change your subject matter. Change your format. If you've been painting big, paint small. If you've been painting landscapes, paint a still life. The point is to keep the hand moving and the eye engaged, even when the heart is not cooperating.

Dry seasons are also invitations to study. Read about painting. Go to a museum. Look at work that moves you and ask yourself why it works. Take a workshop from someone who teaches differently than you do. Study a new medium. The dry season is fallow ground, and fallow ground can be enriched.

What you must not do is quit. Marcus wrote that the soul becomes dyed the color of its thoughts. If your habitual thought during a dry season is "I'm finished," that thought will color everything. If your habitual thought is "This is difficult, and I am still here," that is a different color entirely.

Talk to other artists. You will discover that everyone goes through this. The painter whose work you most admire has had dry seasons that lasted a year. The instructor who seems effortlessly confident has stood in front of a blank canvas and felt nothing. You are not alone. And the fact that every serious artist endures these stretches tells you something important: they are not a sign of failure. They are a feature of the creative life.

One more thing about dry seasons: they often precede breakthroughs. The frustration of not being able to paint the way you used to is sometimes the sign that you are outgrowing your old approach. Your eye has developed faster than your hand. You can see things in nature that your current technique cannot capture, and the gap is making you miserable. This is actually progress, though it feels like regression.

Marcus wrote about the chrysalis, the stage of transformation that looks, from the outside, like death. The caterpillar dissolves before it becomes the butterfly. Your old way of painting may need to dissolve before the new one emerges. This does not feel like growth. It feels like drowning. But if you keep working through it, if you keep making bad paintings and studying them honestly, the new approach will begin to appear. Not all at once, but in glimpses. A stroke here that feels different. A color decision there that surprises you. These are the first signs of spring.

Do not let anyone tell you that a dry season means you should quit. The painters who quit during drought are the ones who needed the external validation of good results to keep going. The painters who survive are the ones whose commitment goes deeper than results. They paint because painting is what they do. The outcome of any single painting is secondary to the practice itself.

Your job during a dry season is the same as your job during a productive one: show up, do the work, remain honest. The results will take care of themselves. They always do.

• • •

Reflections & Journal Prompts

— *Am I currently in a dry season? If so, what small, pressure-free work could I do to keep the hand moving?*

— *What did I learn from my last creative drought that I can apply now?*

— *Is there a fundamentals exercise I could return to that might rebuild my confidence from the ground up?*

— *Can I name one artist I admire who has spoken openly about a difficult creative period?*

• • •

Vincent van Gogh, in the middle of one of the most difficult stretches of his life, no sales, no recognition, fragile health, wrote in a letter, *"What would life be if we had no courage to attempt anything?"* He had every reason to quit. He kept painting. Not because the results were encouraging, but because the work itself was the only honest answer he had to the difficulty. The dry season did not end quickly for Van Gogh. But he never stopped attempting. And the paintings that came out of those hard years changed the course of art.

Winter does not mean the tree is dead. It means the roots are doing their work underground, in the dark, where no one can see. Stay at the easel. Keep painting. Spring will come, and when it does, you will be stronger for having endured the cold.

CHAPTER 12
Quiet Excellence and the Steward's Heart

Character Over Reputation, Offering Over Performance

There is an artist you have never heard of. She paints in a small studio in a town you have never visited. Her work is extraordinary. She will never be famous. She paints anyway.

She may be the finest painter of her generation.

· · ·

Marcus Aurelius drew a sharp line between two things that most people confuse: character and reputation. Character is who you are when no one is looking. Reputation is who other people think you are. Marcus had no illusions about which one matters.

The art world runs on reputation. Gallery placement, social media presence, award lists, magazine features: these are the currencies of visibility. And there is nothing inherently wrong with any of them. Recognition can open doors. It can sustain a career. It can bring your work to people who need to see it.

But when reputation becomes the goal, when you paint for the algorithm, teach for the applause, enter shows for the validation rather than the challenge, something essential dies in the work. The freshness drains out. The story becomes generic. The design starts to serve trends instead of truth.

Marcus would recognize this trap. He wrote about people who live for others' approval, who measure their worth by the opinion of the crowd. He called it a form of slavery. The artist who cannot paint without an audience is in chains, even if the chains are made of gold.

Quiet excellence is the alternative. It is the decision to do excellent work because excellent work is its own justification, because the making of a strong, true painting is a worthy act regardless of who sees it. This is not a rejection of ambition. It is ambition pointed in the right direction: at the quality of the work, not at the noise surrounding it.

We live in a time that confuses visibility with value. The loudest work is often treated as the strongest. The most shared artist is assumed to be the most important. A person can begin to feel that if they are not posting, branding, reacting, and constantly presenting themselves, then they are somehow falling behind. Artists are especially vulnerable to this pressure because art is visual, response is measurable, comparison is easy, and public attention can feel like proof.

The first danger of noise is fragmentation. The artist's attention gets split. Part of the mind is with the painting, but another part is already imagining how the painting will be received. Part is in the studio, another part is in the feed. This weakens presence. And weakened presence weakens the work itself.

It is possible to become well known and underdeveloped. Possible to be frequently seen and inwardly shallow. Possible to be praised for consistency in public while privately repeating oneself from fear. That should sober us.

Some of the best paintings in history were made in obscurity. Some of the worst were made by famous people coasting on reputation. Quality and visibility are separate variables. They can overlap, but they often do not.

For the working artist, this means establishing an internal standard that does not depend on external validation. You know when a painting works. You know when the design is strong, the story is clear, the handling is fresh. You know when you cheated, cut corners, or settled for less than your best. That internal compass is the only one that will never mislead you.

But there is a deeper current running through this chapter, and it connects everything this book has tried to say. At some point, every serious artist must decide what they believe their work finally is. Self-expression alone? A career? A craft? A search for beauty? Or something more.

To speak of stewardship is to say that what you have is not only yours to use, but yours to tend faithfully. Your eye. Your time. Your attention. Your skill. Your taste. Your students. Your years. None of these are self-generated in the fullest sense. They are developed through labor, discipline, failure, study, courage, and long practice, yes. But they are also received.

That is where a deeper humility enters the artist's life. To feel that rightly is not meant to produce panic. It is meant to produce gratitude. I have been given this hour. I have been given these eyes. I have been given these students, these subjects, this season, this measure of strength. What would it mean to answer that gift faithfully?

The artist who sees the work as stewardship rather than self-magnification has a healthier center. They still care about excellence. In fact, they may care more deeply. But they are less possessed by the need to prove themselves through every painting. Their work can become an offering instead of a performance. They can ask not only, "How do I look through this?" but, "What is this asking of me? What deserves to be seen clearly? What can I serve here besides myself?"

Stewardship also helps artists age honestly. If art is mostly ego and appetite, aging can feel like diminishment only. Slower hands, less stamina, fewer years, fewer chances. But if art is stewardship, aging can refine certain things even as others narrow. Vision may deepen. Editing may improve. Tenderness may grow. Teaching may ripen. The work may simplify into truer form.

There is a test you can apply to any creative decision: would I do this if no one were watching? Would I paint this subject, take this risk, spend this afternoon on a study, if I knew the painting would never be seen? If the answer is yes, you are on solid ground. If the answer is no, if the decision is motivated primarily by how it will look to others, then you are serving your reputation instead of your art.

In teaching, quiet excellence means preparing thoroughly for every class, even the ones with four students instead of forty. It means giving your best critique to the beginner who will never become a professional, because she deserves the same respect as the emerging talent. It means judging your teaching by whether the students grew, not by whether they praised you on social media.

There is also a relationship between stewardship and wonder. Artists often begin in wonder. Something catches the eye. Light through sycamores. Mist rising off water. A single lit window at dusk. Cold stone warmed by evening. A bend in the road. A weathered fence. The quiet mercy of ordinary things. But over time, ambition, business, deadlines, comparison, and fatigue can harden the eye. Stewardship helps return the artist to wonder because it teaches that seeing itself is part of the gift. To notice well is not nothing. To be moved is not nothing. To stand before ordinary beauty and still feel gratitude is not childish. It is part of staying alive.

In that sense, making art can become a response to grace. Not in a forced or decorative way. Not with pious varnish. But as a life that keeps saying, through labor and attention: this matters. This is beautiful. This sorrow is worth carrying. This light is worth honoring. This ordinary thing is not empty. This human moment deserves witness. That kind of work blesses people. Not always loudly. Not always obviously. But deeply.

Noisy ambition exhausts you because it makes everything a performance. Quiet excellence sustains you because it makes everything a practice. One is theater. The other is craft. Marcus chose craft. The wisest painters do too.

The art life is not a performance. It is a practice: a daily, lifelong practice of seeing, designing, telling the truth with paint, and serving the subject more than the self. If you do that well, with consistency and honesty and the kind of courage that does not need an audience, you will have lived a creative life worth living. And that is its own reward, whether the world notices or not.

• • •

Reflections & Journal Prompts

— *If no one would ever see my next painting, would I still make it? Would I make the same painting?*

— *Where am I currently letting reputation drive my creative decisions?*

— *Do I have an internal standard for my work that is independent of external feedback?*

— *What would it look like to pursue quiet excellence for the next year?*

• • •

Winslow Homer spent his final years alone on the coast of Maine, painting the sea and the rocks and the weather with a directness that still stops people in galleries a century later. He once said, *"The Sun will not rise, or set, without my notice, and thanks."* No audience. No committee. No social media strategy. Just a painter paying attention to the light and being grateful for the chance to see it. That is stewardship in twelve words. Noticing. Giving thanks. And letting the work be the offering.

The painter who works in silence, with full attention, for the love of the work itself, is the freest artist alive. Reputation comes and goes. The internet forgets in a week. But a painting made with honesty, skill, and clear purpose, offered back as faithful stewardship of a gift received: that is the kind of thing that lasts. Not because anyone notices, but because it is true.

Afterword

A Calm Hand and a Clear Eye

In the end, the artist's life is not built only from talent.

Talent matters, of course. So do skill, taste, discipline, timing, courage, and years of honest work. But none of those fully explain why one artist grows steadier while another grows scattered, why one deepens while another merely stays busy, why one teaches with generosity while another performs, or why one body of work gains weight over time while another remains clever but thin.

The difference is often inward.

Marcus Aurelius understood this well. He knew that a person's real life is shaped not only by what happens around them, but by what they permit to rule within them. For the artist, that inner field matters immensely. Paintings do not come only from the hand. They come through the mind, the temperament, the loves, the order or disorder of the inner room.

The ideas we have walked through are not complicated. Govern your mind. Do the work in front of you. Release what you cannot control. Handle praise and criticism with the same steady eye. Keep your ego in check. Return to the easel with discipline and patience. Simplify. Use your obstacles. Remember that time is short. Teach generously. Endure the dry seasons. Pursue quiet excellence over noisy ambition. See your work as stewardship, not self-magnification.

None of these are new ideas. They are old ideas, some of the oldest useful ideas in human civilization. But old does not mean outdated. It means tested. These principles have survived two thousand years because they work. They worked for a Roman emperor fighting to stay sane in an impossible job. They work for a painter standing at an easel trying to make something true.

Design gives clarity. Story gives meaning. Freshness gives life. These three ideas will serve you in every painting you make and every day you live as an artist. They are practical. They are portable. They work under pressure. And they echo the stoic conviction that a well-ordered life is a life of purpose, attention, and honest work.

If this book has done its job, you will not remember every chapter. But you will remember a feeling: the sense that it is possible to build an art life that is both ambitious and peaceful, both disciplined and free, both honest and kind. That it is possible to paint with courage without needing to be fearless. To teach with authority without needing to be right. To pursue excellence without needing to be praised.

Wonder matters more than most serious people allow. Many artists begin in wonder and then slowly trade it for ambition, pressure, comparison, and overproduction. But the best work usually keeps some wonder alive. Not naivete. Not sentimentality. Wonder. The capacity to be struck by light through sycamores, by a figure against shadow, by mist lifting from water, by the endurance in an old tree, by the warmth of one lit window in a cold street. Wonder slows the eye down. It opens story. It deepens gratitude. It reminds the artist that seeing is itself part of the gift.

Go back to the studio. Pick up the brush. Paint the truth of what you see. Let the rest take care of itself.

You have an easel, a subject, a set of brushes, and the accumulated wisdom of every painting you have ever made. You have your eye, which sees things no one else sees the way you see them. You have your hands, which know things your mind has not yet articulated. And you have today, this one day, with its particular light and its particular demands.

That is enough. It has always been enough.

The light is moving. It always is.

• • •

Claude Monet, looking back near the end of a long life of painting, said, *"I perhaps owe having become a painter to flowers."* Not to ambition. Not to technique. Not to the market or the critics or the Salon. To flowers. To the thing that first stopped him and made him look. Wonder came before everything else. It still does, for any painter honest enough to remember where the whole thing started.

Appendix

Twenty Stoic Reminders for Artists

Field notes for the studio wall, the sketchbook, or the hard morning before you pick up the brush.

1	Govern the mind before touching the brush.
2	Do the work in front of you, not the career in your imagination.
3	You cannot control the jury, the gallery, the market, or the weather. Paint anyway.
4	Praise is pleasant. It is not a compass.
5	Criticism may contain truth, but it is not your identity.
6	Ego says the painting is about you. It is not. It is about the light, the story, the truth of what you saw.
7	Show up. Mix paint. Begin. Inspiration follows action.
8	What you leave out is part of what you say. Simplify the design. Simplify the palette. Simplify the story.
9	Failed paintings are your best teachers. Study them without defensiveness.
10	Constraints are allies. A limited palette, a time limit, counted brush-strokes, a small canvas: these produce focus, not limitation.
11	Your time is finite. Paint the subjects that move you, not the ones that seem safe.
12	Teach to help, not to impress. The student needs the next right step, not everything you know.
13	The dry season is not failure. It is winter. Keep the roots fed.
14	Do not compare your daily effort to someone else's best exhibition piece. You are seeing two different things.
15	One clean stroke is worth ten hesitant ones. Trust your eye. Commit. Then leave it alone.
16	Do not confuse visibility with depth. Quiet work done faithfully is never wasted.
17	The first principles never change: value, shape, edges, color, design. Return to them constantly.

18	Have an abundance mentality. Scarcity thinking poisons the art community. There is always enough room for another good painter. Encourage freely. Share what you know. The gift grows by being given away, not guarded.
19	Your gifts are real. They are also entrusted. Tend them.
20	The light is moving. It is always moving. Get to work.

About the Author

Steve Puttrich is a painter, instructor, and inventor based in Holland, Michigan. He trained at the American Academy of Art and the School of the Art Institute of Chicago, spent years as a creative director, and eventually did what he was made to do: paint full time and teach others to see.

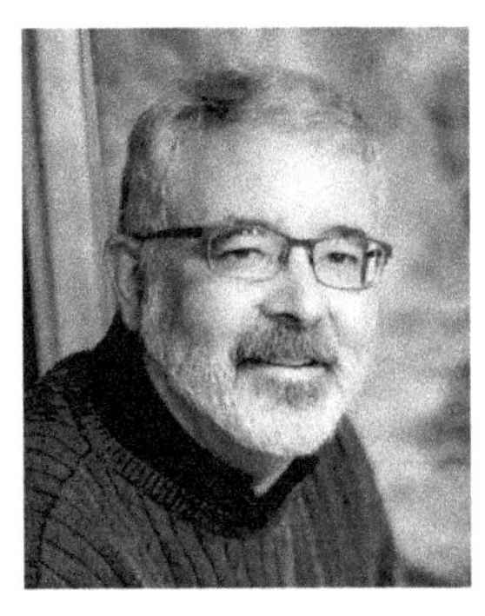

He paints woodland scenes, waterfalls, and forest light at his home studio in Marigold Woods, and teaches oil painting, watercolor, and plein air workshops at venues across the country, including the Palette and Chisel Academy of Fine Arts, Scottsdale Artists' School, Madeline Island School of Arts, and the Plein Air Convention and Expo (PACE). His teaching framework, Design gives clarity, Story gives meaning, Freshness gives life, runs through everything he does.

Steve is the inventor of the Fairview Finder, a precision viewfinder and composition tool for painters, and the founder of Fairview & Evergreen, LLC. He has been married to Bobbie for forty-three years. They have three grown children who are now making light of their own.

He still drags his stone-cold corpse to the easel most mornings. And life still meets him there.

More information on art, workshops and resource materials can be found here:

www.steveputtrich.com

www.FairviewFinder.com

www.ingramcontent.com/pod-product-compliance
Lightning Source LLC
Chambersburg PA
CBHW040131150726
48005CB00015B/2458